Min
7 Quick Steps to
F

HowExpert Press & Dena Gray

Copyright <u>HowExpert.com</u>

Table of Contents

1. INTRODUCTION 3
2. CENTRAL MAUI 11
3. SOUTH MAUI 19
4. WEST MAUI 33
5. UPCOUNTRY MAUI AND HALEAKALA 46
6. ROAD TO HANA AND SOUTHEAST MAUI 50
7. MAUI ACTIVITIES AND ADVENTURES 54
About the Expert 57

Step 1. INTRODUCTION

Maui Nō Ka 'Oi

In Maui, we have a saying – "Maui Nō Ka 'Oi" – which means "Maui is the best!" The second-largest of the Hawaiian Islands, Maui is the perfect blend of unspoiled tropical paradise and luxury resort destination. Nicknamed "The Valley Isle" due to the luscious green valley resting between its two volcanoes, Haleakala and Mauna Kahalawai (West Maui Mountains), Maui is best known for its natural beauty and its spirit of "aloha." Stunning beaches, mystic jungle waterfalls, bamboo forests, waving fields of sugar cane, whales breaching in the crystal blue ocean, sunrise over a volcano – all these sights and more await the visitor to Maui. Honeymooners, golfers, sports enthusiasts, and families with small children can all find the perfect vacation destination here.

The Hawaiian Islands were first settled by voyagers from the Marquesas Islands, a group of volcanic islands 2,000 miles away in French Polynesia. According to Hawaiian tradition, Hawai'iloa was the navigator on that first journey, and named the island of Maui after his son (who had himself been named for the demigod Maui). Oahu and Kauai were similarly named after his other sons, while the Big Island of Hawai'i was named after Hawai'iloa himself.

The original settlers of the Hawaiian Islands populated the islands for 600-800 years before the Tahitians arrived around the year 1200. These settlers may have been the Menehune (little people) of legend. The word Menehune comes from the Tahitian word "manahune" – meaning commoner – and may refer to a race of people who were considered lesser in social status, rather than being significantly small in stature. The Menehune were said to be skilled master craftsmen, who built heiau (temples), fishponds, and other structures, some of which can still be seen today on Kauai and Oahu.

The first westerner to arrive in the Hawaiian Islands was an Englishman named Captain James Cook, who made landfall in Kauai in 1778. Captain Cook didn't land on Maui because the surf was too high and he couldn't find a harbor. During his third visit to the Hawaiian Islands, an altercation broke out and Cook was killed in the melee. He died in 1779 at the age of 51, on the Big Island at Kealakakua Bay. In 1786, Jean-Francois de Galaup La Pérouse was the first European to actually set foot on Maui, making landing in the area now known as La Perouse Bay.

King Kamehameha I of the Big Island invaded Maui in 1795, and by 1810 he had united the entire archipelago into one kingdom. During these years, several contagious diseases decimated the Hawaiian population, which was estimated at somewhere between 250,000 to 1 million people when Europeans first arrived in 1779. As a consequence of European contact and exposure to measles, cholera, and gonorrhea, by 1848 the number of remaining Hawaiians numbered only around 88,000. In 1893, approximately 100 years after Maui became part of a united Hawaii, the kingdom was overthrown by United States businessmen on the island of Oahu, leading to the annexation of the islands to the United States in 1898. In 1896, the Hawaiian language was banned from schools and government offices and would not be allowed in schools for the next 40 years.

Hawaii officially became the 50th state in 1959.

Maui Weather and Geography

Maui weather varies more by location than by season, due to its micro-climates. Each area has its own distinctive climate. At any given time, it is likely to be raining somewhere on Maui, and sunny in another location – maybe only a few miles apart! If at any time you don't like the weather in Maui, you can get in your car and drive for a few minutes to find weather more to your liking.

The dominant feature of Maui, Haleakala Volcano, is considered the world's largest dormant volcano and is believed to have erupted last in 1786. The summit of Haleakala gets very cold, while temperatures are usually warmer at sea level.

Overall, Maui's daytime temperatures average between 75 and 90 degrees Fahrenheit year round, with evening temperatures dropping by about 15 to 18 degrees. The weather can be quite variable even within these micro-climates, so you may need to be flexible with your plans if the weather isn't cooperating. Swap a windy beach day for a bamboo forest hike, rather than spend the day dodging blasts of sand in your face!

Central Maui (Kahului, Wailuku) tends to be hot throughout the year. Kahului can be at times muggy, but doesn't actually get a lot of rain. Wailuku gets more rain than Kahului, since it is closer to the West Maui Mountains.

South Maui (Kihei, Wailea, Makena) and West Maui (Lahaina, Ka'anapali, Kapalua) are both commonly dry and hot, up to 92 degrees. If it's raining in these areas, it may be raining over the entire island! In these areas you will find tropical flowers that do best in drier climates, such as hibiscus and plumeria.

The North Shore (Haiku, Paia) and East Maui (Ke'anae, Hana and Kipahulu) get significantly more rain, especially at higher elevations. These areas are therefore lush and covered in thick vegetation, including tropical flowers that thrive in wet conditions, such as ginger, heliconia, and anthurium. Haiku has measurable rain approximately 204 days per year. The O'heo Gulch Pools area of Kipahulu has measurable rainfall an astonishing 270 days per year! A popular saying in Maui is, "No rain, no rainbows."

Upcountry Maui usually has warm temperatures during the day, with cooler evenings. The higher up Haleakala you venture, the cooler the temperatures, especially at night or early morning. Kula can get as cold as 40 degrees in the wee hours, and the summit of Haleakala can have freezing temperatures and even snow on rare occasions!

Occasionally Maui gets "Kona" winds or storms, meaning southwesterly winds (opposite direction of the usual trade winds). Kona storms sometimes bring rainfall to the South and West areas of Maui that are typically hot and dry. The Kona winds can also bring VOG, harmful volcanic air pollution, emitted from the Big Island's Kilauea volcano.

Important Information for Visitors

When visiting a new area, it's important to learn about and respect the local culture. Here are some tips for visiting Maui:
1. Respect the aina (land). Please clean up after yourself and don't litter. Keep a distance from sea turtles, monk seals, and humpback whales. They are endangered species and are protected by law, with hefty fines. Also, don't step on or

touch coral reefs. "Reef-safe" sunscreen will also help make sure Maui's reefs are protected and are still here when you next visit. Watch for Marine Life Conservation District signs. These areas do not allow fishing, nor the taking of any natural resources (including marine life, rocks, or shells). Your kokua (careful consideration) is appreciated.

2. Always remove your shoes before entering someone's home.
3. When taking a leisurely drive, if you notice a local driver behind you, pull off the road to your right as soon as it is safe to do so, and let the local person pass. They are probably on the way to work and will be extremely grateful not to drive at a sightseeing pace!
4. You may hear the word "haole" (pronounced how-lee), which is the Hawaiian word for foreigner and is not generally meant disrespectfully. It simply means "someone unfamiliar."
5. Note "KAPU" signs and stay out of these forbidden areas. The Tahitians introduced the kapu system, a strict code of conduct and religious law system with thousands of rules. The kapu system was the core of Hawaiian culture until it was abolished in 1819. Kapu means "restricted," and to this day the word is often used to mean "No Trespassing" on signs throughout Hawaii.
6. In Hawaii, gratuities are expected in accordance with American standards. In restaurants, the customary tip is 15-20% of the total bill. Please tip according to these customs, as many workers in Hawaii are paid less than

minimum wage (tips are factored into their regular pay in accordance with local law). The workers and their families depend on tips to put food on their own tables.
7. In Hawaii, many locals speak "Pidgin," an officially recognized language that originated on sugarcane plantations as a form of communication between Hawaiians, immigrants from several different countries, and English speakers. Don't assume that someone speaking Pidgin is uneducated. Most locals speak perfect English as well as Pidgin! Some locals recommend that visitors don't attempt to speak Pidgin as it may be considered rude.
8. When presented with a lei, accept it and wear it gracefully by centering it on your shoulders rather than on your neck. It is considered impolite to take a lei off in front of the person who gave it to you.
9. Treat all sacred sites with extreme respect. Avoid loud or disruptive behavior, immodest clothing, and even photography at these sacred sites. Offerings are not required, and silent reverence is the best behavior. Your mindfulness is appreciated, as Hawaiian culture and history is of utmost importance to Hawaii's locals, especially as it seems to be disappearing before their very eyes.
10. Have a spirit of "aloha" – a positive and flexible attitude, mindfulness, and friendliness. You will blend in well with a spirit of aloha, because Maui locals have it in abundance!

Beach Safety

Please remember that all beaches in Maui have potential dangers. Never swim alone. Heed all "Hazard" signs on beaches (they are black, yellow and orange). Take stock of the ocean conditions before deciding whether to enter the water, and as the saying goes, "When in doubt, don't go out." Don't dive into shallow waves or waters of unknown depth. Never turn your back on the ocean, even when walking on the beach – waves come in sets, and waves of unexpectedly large size do occur. Apply (and reapply!) "reef-safe" sunburn protection. All Hawaii beaches and oceans may be inhabited by sharks, jellyfish, sea urchins, and other creatures that may cause harm.

Sharks rarely attack humans, and when they do it is usually out of confusion or curiosity. They prefer turtles, seals, or fish as their food. But don't swim at night or twilight, nor in murky waters where sharks may mistake you for their natural prey. Don't swim near runoff into the ocean, or near active fishermen, as these are attractive places for sharks to find a meal. Don't enter the water if you are bleeding or have a cut or open wound, as the scent of blood attracts sharks from up to a mile away. Similarly, urinating in the ocean may attract sharks. Avoid wearing bright, high-contrast colors or sparkling jewelry in the water. That said, please keep in mind that even with millions of people enjoying the ocean around Maui every year, shark incidents are rare. The entire state of Hawaii only averages about 4 shark incidents per year, almost always non-fatal. Your chances of being attacked by a shark while visiting Maui are actually slim to none.

Additional Safety Information

Don't leave anything highly valuable unattended on the beach or even in your car. Car break-ins are the number one crime in Maui.

Expect to encounter critters! Cockroaches, large cockroaches, and even larger cockroaches. Centipedes and scorpions. Cane spiders the size of your hand (they're harmless though!). The good news is, none of these critters you may encounter on Maui have bites or stings that are deadly. Usually the worst damage you'll get from one of these insects is little worse than a bee sting. Mosquitoes abound so you'll want to wear natural insect repellent – but rest assured that dengue fever, chikungunya, and similar viral outbreaks have NOT been reported on Maui.

Never swim in freshwater ponds or waterfalls if you have an open sore or cut, as these waters may potentially contain waterborne bacteria – especially after runoff has entered the water from heavy rains. You take a risk whenever swimming directly below a waterfall, because natural debris such as large tree branches can fall right on top of unsuspecting swimmers below.

While keeping these safety tips in mind is a good idea, remember that everything in life involves a certain amount of risk. A Hawaiian proverb: 'Oi kau ka lau, E hana I ola Honua... "Live your life while the sun is still shining."

Step 2. CENTRAL MAUI

KAHULUI

Kahului is the home of Maui's main airport (Kahului Airport) and also its main seaport, used for shipping and for docking of cruise ships. Kahului is the largest city in Maui and is also the retail center for residents, with several shopping centers and malls. All the "big box" stores in Maui (Costco, Walmart, Target, etc.) are located in Kahului. It is the home of the Kahului Community College campus and also the Maui Arts and Cultural Center, where concerts and other performances occur. The Maui Swap Meet in Kahului is an excellent place to buy souvenirs, art, local-made sunburn remedies, and gifts for friends and family back home. Many of the over 200 vendors are artists who craft the products themselves, and sell their wares at the swap meet every Saturday from 7am to 1pm.

Kahului was established in the 1850s by Henry Baldwin and Samuel Alexander as part of their sugar growing operations. While Kahului is generally considered to be more of a business hub than a tourist destination, it does offer sights such as the Alexander & Baldwin Sugar Museum, Kanaha Pond State Wildlife Sanctuary, and Kanaha Beach Park.

WAILUKU

Wailuku is located 10 minutes west of Kahului and is the county seat of government for Maui. Wailuku also has shopping and residential areas, but there are few hotels in the area. Market Street is a quaint shopping location with many "mom and pop" family businesses, some that have been in operation for generations. The wooden storefronts and the aloha you encounter here can take you back in time as you meander through Wailuku's shops, bakeries, and restaurants.

There are two ancient Hawaiian "heiau" (temples) near Wailuku. The Haleki'i Heiau and the Pihana Heiau are some of the most accessible remaining Hawaiian structures from pre-European contact times. They are located about a quarter mile inland along the west side of Iao Stream. Legend says the menehune constructed both of these heiau within a single night, utilizing rock from nearby Paukukalo Beach.

Wailuku has several other historic sites, such as the Iao Theater built in 1927, the Ka'ahumanu Church (named after Queen Ka'ahumanu) which was built in 1876, and the Bailey House or "Hale Hoikeike" (House of Display), a former seminary and home built in 1833 that now serves as a museum. The Bailey House contains Hawaiian history displays, and native Hawaiian plants are cultivated on the grounds surrounding it.

The Maui Tropical Plantation is minutes away in Waikapu, and has free admission to its beautiful grounds with a stunning view of the gorgeous Waikapu valley. Experience a ziplining adventure, have dinner in its restaurant, and learn about its 30 year history as productive, working plantation with over 40 crops and hundreds of tropical and native plants.

Paia

Paia is located where Central Maui meets the island's North Shore. Alexander & Baldwin established the Paia Sugar Mill in the late 1800s, and immigrant workers from around the world were brought in to live and work in Paia. Camps to house workers at the Paia Sugar Mill were quickly constructed. The area became a bustling community and by 1896, Paia Town was officially born with the opening of the Paia Store. Over time, more stores, schools, a movie theater and a hospital were built to support the growing population.

By the 1950s, sugar production was in decline and plantation workers began to move out of the camps and into newly-built homes in the nearby developing areas of Kahului and Wailuku. In 2000, the Paia Sugar Mill officially closed. In 2016, Maui's last remaining sugar plantation, Hawaiian Commercial and Sugar (HC&S), announced that it would cease growing sugar on the 36,000 acres that had been devoted to sugar cane. This represents a big change for Paia, and indeed for all of Maui, where the familiar view of waving sugar cane fields is one of its defining features.

Paia experienced another boom in the 1960s and 1970s, as hippies and free-thinkers flocked to this laid-back coastal town and put down roots. Windsurfing became popular in the 1980s and 1990s as adventurers from around the world discovered the perfect conditions for windsurfing at Ho'okipa Beach Park in Paia. Paia is now known as the "Windsurfing Capital of the World" as well as the quaint country/hippie town on Maui's North Shore.

CENTRAL MAUI BEACHES

Please remember that all beaches in Maui have potential dangers. For more tips on beach safety, please read the section titled, "Important Information for Visitors."

KAHULUI BEACHES

Kanaha Beach Park

One mile long Kanaha Beach Park is the only beach in Kahului, and is located directly next to the Kahului Airport. The beach has lawns and shade trees as well as pale golden sand. It is frequently very windy, and is a world-class windsurfing and kite boarding spot, appropriate for both beginners and experts. The colorful sails of windsurfers are a beautiful contrast to the sea and sand. Stand-up paddle boarders are also a common sight in Kanaha Beach Park on mornings before the winds kick up.

Although Kanaha Beach Park is best known for kite boarding and windsurfing, the beach also has three marked swimming areas that are protected by ropes. These three shallow, calm swimming coves are good for families with small children – but there are far better beaches to be enjoyed in South Maui and West Maui.

<u>Location:</u> Amala Place, Kahului
<u>Amenities:</u>
- Restrooms
- Shower
- Picnic area

WAILUKU BEACHES

Waiehu Beach Park and Waihee Beach Park

These two beach parks are gathering place for locals and windsurfers. These are not the best beaches for swimming or sunbathing, due to abundant seaweed and windy conditions.

Location: Lower Waiehu Beach Road, Wailuku and Halewaiu Road, Wailuku

Amenities:
- Restrooms
- Shower
- Picnic area

PAIA BEACHES

Ho'okipa Beach Park

Ho'okipa Beach Park is possibly the most renowned windsurfing beach in the world. Before you surf or sail here, double-check that the conditions are a match to your skill level – particularly if the surf is big. Ho'okipa has strong winds, rip currents and a shallow reef. If you're a beginner, consider windsurfing at Kanaha instead of Ho'okipa.

Ho'okipa Lookout is on the edge of a cliff overlooking the beach. This is a great place to be able to see all the action without getting in the mix of it. The Ho'okipa Lookout is also a great place to spot honu (Hawaiian green sea turtles) and whales during whale season (December-April).

Location: Mile Marker 9, Hana Highway, Paia

Amenities:
- Restrooms
- Shower
- Lifeguard

- Picnic area

Lower Paia Park

Lower Paia Park is an good beach for surfing. Boogie-boarders and windsurfers also take advantage of the shorebreak at Lower Paia Park. This is not really a good beach for snorkeling or swimming, especially in the afternoon when the winds pick up.

Location: Hana Highway between Baldwin Beach Park and Paia Town

Amenities:
- Restrooms
- Shower
- Lifeguard
- Picnic area

H.A. Baldwin Beach Park

H.A. Baldwin Beach Park is a long, sandy, beautiful beach and is amazing for walking, running, sunbathing, surfing, body surfing, kite surfing, and more. There are plenty of shade trees and grassy areas for relaxing as well. The water at Baldwin Beach can sometimes be a bit murky. Novice swimmers should be cautious as the seafloor drops off relatively quickly, causing a shorebreak that can be rough.

Location: Hana Highway between Maui Country Club and Paia

Amenities:
- Restrooms
- Shower
- Lifeguard
- Picnic area

Spreckelsville Beach
Spreckelsville Beach is the collective name of this two mile stretch of smaller beaches (Camp One, Sprecks Beach, Lobster Cove, Sugar Cove and Baby Beach). These beaches are mainly used by windsurfers and fishermen due to cloudy water, strong currents, and near-constant winds.
Location: Mile Marker 5 (Baby Beach), Hana Highway, Paia
Amenities:
- No facilities

Tavares Beach
Tavares Beach is a sandy white beach shaped like a crescent in Kuau, right next to Paia. This beautiful beach is good for swimming, snorkeling, surfing, windsurfing, and spearfishing and is popular with locals.
Location: Half a mile past Paia on Hana Highway
Amenities:
- No facilities

CENTRAL MAUI SIGHTS, SHOPPING, AND DINING

Recommended Sights:
- Alexander & Baldwin Sugar Museum - 3957 Hansen Road, Kahului
- Iao Valley State Park and the Iao Needle - 54 South High Street, Wailuku
- Maui Tropical Plantation - 1670 Honoapi'ilani Highway, Wailuku

- Bailey House - 2375 Main Street, Wailuku
- Ho'okipa Lookout - Mile Marker 9, Hana Highway, Paia

Recommended Shopping:
- Maui Swap Meet (Saturday mornings) - 310 West Ka'ahumanu Avenue, Kahului
- Maui Tropix (Maui Built) - 261 Dairy Road, Kahului
- Market Street (local favorite shops) - Market Street, Wailuku
- Paia Town (gifts, souvenirs, artworks, clothing and more) - Hana Highway, Paia

Recommended Dining:
- Da Kitchen (local style food) - 425 Koloa Street, Kahului
- Ululani's Hawaiian Shave Ice (voted #1 shave ice) - 333 Dairy Road, Kahului
- Aria's Restaurant & Catering (fine dining) - 2062 West Vineyard Street, Wailuku
- Flatbread Company (flatbread pizza with local ingredients) - 89 Hana Highway, Paia
- Paia Fish Market (casual dining, fresh fish) - 100 Baldwin Avenue, Paia
- Mama's Fish House (finest dining) - 799 Poho Place, Paia

Step 3. SOUTH MAUI

KIHEI

Kihei is one of the most popular destinations for visitors to Maui, due in part to the relative affordability of its condos, cottages, and hotel rooms. With over six miles of beautiful beaches and a plethora of restaurants and shops to choose from, it's easy to see why so many visitors choose to make Kihei their base when planning a stay on Maui.

The area was originally called Kama'ole – meaning "barren" in Hawaiian – due to its hot temperatures and infrequent rain (typically less than 13 inches of rain per year). Due to lack of water, Kihei was sparsely populated up until the 1960s. Historically, those native Hawaiians who did settle here relied mainly on fishing or harvesting kiawe (mesquite), and traded these for items that wouldn't grow in the area's desert climate.

Once water was rerouted down to Kihei from Central and West Maui in the 1960s, the area began to be rapidly (and randomly) developed with hotels and resorts to attract visitors. With an average of 276 days of sunshine per year, the consistent warm weather and sandy beaches make Kihei a perfect vacation spot. Kihei does get strong afternoon winds on most days, so you'll want to get to the beach early. The easy appeal of this beach town with access to restaurants, bars, shopping, small businesses, and ocean activities has made it a permanent home to approximately 20,000 residents.

WAILEA

Wailea is a gorgeous resort community with five stunning crescent-shaped beaches and beautifully landscaped luxury hotels. Spanning approximately 1,500 acres, the Wailea Resort was a master planned development, unlike Kihei, which sprang up more spontaneously. The weather in Wailea is also cooler than in Kihei, with less vigorous afternoon winds.

Wailea means "Waters of Lea." According to legend, Lea was the Hawaiian goddess of canoe builders. She would appear in the form of an elepaio bird (forest bird) and would fly over this area, watching over the canoe builders as they worked. Lea would also assist in finding the best koa wood trees to be used for canoe building, by pecking on the trees and revealing which trees were hollow and which were solid.

Many of the best beaches on Maui are connected by the Wailea Beach Path, allowing visitors to walk from one resort to another while enjoying unparalleled views of West Maui, Lanai, Kaho'olawe and Molokini. The one and a half miles of heavenly shoreline connected by the walkway are a great place to spot honu (green sea turtles) and also humpback whales during whale season (November through May). Best of all, the Wailea Beach Path is free to the public and easy to access!

In addition to its top-notch beaches, Wailea has high-end shopping, restaurants, and golf courses. Visitors to Maui desiring a relaxing, upscale resort vacation (while staying close to the action and nightlife of Kihei and Kahului) will be drawn to Wailea.

MAKENA

The area of Makena is home to spectacular

unspoiled beaches. While the weather in Makena is generally warm, this area gets more cloud cover and has fewer sunny days per year than Kihei or Wailea. The name Makena comes from the Hawaiian word "mak'ke" meaning "many gathered."

The dormant cinder cone Pu'u Ola'i (Earthquake Hill) in Makena State Park is a natural formation measuring 360 feet tall that overlooks these world-famous, natural Makena beaches. Pu'u Ola'i was formed by a lava flow and earthquake (possibly in the year 1786). At the base of Pu'u Ola'i, tidepools and lava formations divide the shoreline in two, with Big Beach on one side and Little Beach on the other.

Ahihi-Kinau Natural Area Reserve is located approximately 4 miles past Makena. It has 2,000 protected acres and also the remains of an ancient Hawaiian fishing village, but has been closed to the public since 2008 due to the natural resources being impacted by visitors. La Perouse Bay is located within the Reserve as well.

Hawaiian culture and history are revealed in Makena's ancient fishponds, heiau (temples), and ko'a. Please treat these sites with the utmost respect, and only visit these areas if they are publicly accessible.

One of Makena's most popular resorts for 30 years, the Makena Beach & Golf Resort (formerly the Maui Prince Hotel) closed its doors in July of 2016. The property will be redeveloped into the Makena Golf & Beach Club, a private beachfront community and golf club.

SOUTH MAUI BEACHES AND MOLOKINI

Please remember that all beaches in Maui have potential dangers. For more tips on beach safety, please read the section titled, "Important Information for Visitors."

KIHEI BEACHES

Sugar Beach

As you might guess, Sugar Beach in North Kihei has fine, powdery, pale sand; however, the beach actually got its name from the wharf that was built here in 1899 to service the Kihei Sugar Plantation. It is a popular beach for long walks at sunset. Swimming and snorkeling at Sugar Beach are also possible, however, caution is advised as the reef is not far from shore and can be challenging.
Location: North Kihei Road, Kihei
Amenities:
- Portable toilet

Maipoina Oe Iau Beach Park

Located in North Kihei, this beach is good for windsurfing in the afternoons, as it can be very windy. Maipoina Oe Iau is also an excellent spot for birdwatching.
Location: South Kihei Road, Kihei
Amenities:
- No facilities

Waipu'ilani Park (Kihei Beach Reserve)

Waipu'ilani is a long beach protected by reef. While it is can be suitable for offshore swimming, it sometimes has a lot of seaweed. Stand up paddle boarding can be enjoyable when the winds are minimal. This beach park also has a tennis court and a volleyball court, as

well as grass lawns and areas of shade, ideal for a picnic.
Location: South Kihei Road, Kihei
Amenities:
- Restrooms
- Picnic area

Kalama Beach Park

This North Kihei beach park is most suitable for events and gatherings. Kalama has a fairly small and rocky beach, but it has wide open grassy areas, a basketball and tennis court, a baseball and soccer field, areas for skating and skateboarding, and a playground for children.
Location: South Kihei Road and Keala Place, Kihei
Amenities:
- Restrooms
- Shower
- Picnic area

Cove Park

Cove Park is a small, sandy beach often used for surfing lessons, but is not a great beach for swimming as the water is often full of seaweed.
Location: Iliili Road, Kihei
Amenities:
- Portable toilet
- Boat ramp
- Picnic area

Kama'ole Beach Park I (Kam I)

All three of the "Kam" beaches are

located on South Kihei Road and are usually great for swimming. Kam I is a wide beach with fine sand, and has good snorkeling near the rocky points at its edges. The north end of Kam I is known as "Charley Young Beach," and is often less crowded (thus, popular with locals).
Location: South Kihei Road, Kihei
Amenities:
- Restrooms
- Shower
- Lifeguard

Kama'ole Beach Park II (Kam II)
Kam II is a well-kept and clean beach, similar to the other two Kam beaches, with restaurants right across the street to grab lunch or a drink. After storms the water can be full of lava rock, in which case you may want to choose another beach.
Location: South Kihei Road, Kihei
Amenities:
- Shower
- Lifeguard
- Picnic area

Kama'ole Beach Park III (Kam III)
Kam III has a larger break than the other two Kam beaches, and is therefore the best of the three for boogie-boarding. While a shorter beach than the others, it has nice facilities available and is arguably the most popular Kihei beach.
Location: South Kihei Road, Kihei
Amenities:
- Portable toilets

- Shower
- Picnic area

Keawakapu Beach

This beautiful beach with soft sand is not as well known as other beaches and is therefore less crowded. The sun shines on Keawakapu almost every day of the year, as this area has some of the driest weather on the island. Here you will enjoy swimming, snorkeling and in-season whale watching, along with stunning sunrises and sunsets.

Location: South Kihei Road, Kihei
Amenities:
- Shower

WAILEA BEACHES

Mokapu Beach and Ulua Beach

Calm waters and small waves make these two adjacent beaches perfect for families. They also provide some of the best opportunities for snorkeling on Maui. The water is clearest and best for snorkeling early in the day. As with most Maui beaches, the wind generally kicks up in the afternoons. Mokapu is more picturesque than Ulua, and is usually less crowded.

Location: Ulua Beach Road, Wailea
Amenities:
- Restrooms
- Shower

Wailea Beach

Wailea Beach has crystal clear water and

fine sand, and is considered one of the world's best beaches. However, because it is picturesque and easily accessible, Wailea Beach can also be crowded. Snorkeling here may reveal a variety of tropical fish, including humuhumunukunukuapua'a, the Hawaiian state fish. Don't be surprised if a honu (Hawaiian green sea turtle) pops its head up to say hello while you are swimming!
Location: Wailea Alanui Drive, Wailea (between Grand Wailea and Four Seasons)
Amenities:
- Shower
- Restrooms

Polo Beach Park
This sandy beach with clear water is enjoyable for the whole family. Polo Beach is located right in front of the Kea Lani Resort and is a popular snorkeling destination.
Location: Makena Road, Wailea (in front of Fairmont Kea Lani Hotel)
Amenities:
- Restrooms
- Shower
- Picnic area

Po'olenalena Park
Po'olenalena is one of the less crowded beaches in the Wailea/Makena area, but not because it lacks in beauty or easy access. The snorkeling here is excellent, with sea turtles and tropical fish in abundance. Boogie-boarding is popular here during south swells. Swimming in the clear waters of Po'olenalena

will make you never want to leave Maui!
<u>Location:</u> Makena Alanui Drive, Wailea (Between Wailea Golf Club and Makena Surf)
<u>Amenities:</u>
- Portable toilet

MAKENA BEACHES

Chang's Beach and 5 Caves / 5 Graves (Ulupikanui Beach and Pamolepo)
Chang's Beach is ideal for snorkeling or diving, more than for swimming. This beach also has large underwater caves that should only be explored by the most experienced divers. This area is known as 5 Caves / 5 Graves (named for the underwater caves and also for the nearby cemetery).
<u>Location:</u> Makena Road, Makena
<u>Amenities:</u>
- No facilities

Palauea Beach (White Rock)
White Rock is a tranquil, uncrowded, lesser-known beach because it is tucked away in a mostly residential area. This beach is very good for swimming and snorkeling. The afternoon wind is not as strong here as in many other areas. When the water is calm, this is an excellent beach for families with small children.
<u>Location:</u> Makena Road, Makena
<u>Amenities:</u>
- No facilities

Maluaka Beach
This wide, beautiful beach with pale

golden sand is excellent for swimming and snorkeling and is more protected from the trade winds than most South Maui beaches. The grassy areas make this location one the whole family can enjoy.

Location: Makena Road, Makena (North of White Rock Beach)

Amenities:
- Restrooms
- Showers
- Picnic area

Big Beach (Makena Beach)

Considered by many as the quintessential beach on Maui, Big Beach is expansive and unspoiled. The half-mile long crescent of sand is unusually wide for a Maui beach, which helps it feel uncrowded. While this can be a great spot for experienced swimmers and boogie-boarders, the waves can be large and strong, so Big Beach is not appropriate for small children or beginners.

Location: Makena Road, Makena

Amenities:
- Portable toilet
- Lifeguard
- Picnic area

Little Beach

Little Beach definitely has a relaxed vibe! Although public nudity is illegal in Hawaii, Little Beach patrons seem willing to take their chances. This unofficial "nude beach" of Maui has a drum circle and fire dancing on Sunday evenings. The lava outcropping that separates

Big Beach from Little Beach keeps this area somewhat secluded. Swimming, snorkeling, and boogie-boarding are popular activities at this spot.
Location: Wailea Alanui Road, Makena
Amenities:
- Portable toilet (near Big Beach parking lot)

Makena Landing Beach Park
Makena Landing is a pretty, rustic beach that is good for launching kayaks, fishing, and scuba dives. It it usually a tranquil beach with minimal waves and can be appropriate for small children. There is a shallow reef and plenty of sea life, so Makena Landing can be a nice beach for learning to snorkel if conditions permit.
Location: Makena Road, Makena
Amenities:
- No facilities

Oneuli Black Sand Beach
This pretty black sand beach is unusual and picturesque, but has rough sand and sometimes strong currents. Black sand is made up of ground lava, rather than ground shells and coral like typical white sands, and it's not as comfortable to sit or walk on. Snorkeling at Oneuli can be excellent. Once you get past the rocky entry into the ocean, you'll find coral reefs and abundant sea life.
Location: Wailea Alanui Drive, Makena
Amenities:
- No facilities

Pa'ako Beach (Secret Cove)

Pa'ako Beach is located just south of Big Beach and is a popular spot for weddings due to its rugged beauty. However, this beach is not the easiest to access. This small, sandy cove has excellent swimming when the sea is calm, but most people come here for the gorgeous views of Kaho'olawe and Molokini.

<u>Location:</u> Makena Road, Makena (south of Big Beach)
<u>Amenities:</u>
- No facilities

Molokini

Molokini (also known as Molokini Crater) is a crescent-shaped islet that is actually a partially submerged volcanic crater. As the island of Maui moved over hot spots in the Earth's tectonic plates, the crater was formed. The protected reef inside the crater makes for world-class snorkeling and diving with a wide variety of sea life. The crescent shape protects snorkelers from waves and the waters are very clear, with visibility up to 150 feet deep.

According to one Hawaiian legend, Molokini was a rival of Pele, the fire goddess. Both Molokini and Pele were in love with the same prince. Jealous Pele took her revenge by cutting Molokini in half and turning her to stone. The head of her body became Pu'u Olai, the cinder cone hill on the north end of Makena Beach, and her body became Molokini Crater.

Small tour boats transport snorkelers and divers from Ma'alaea Harbor or Kihei boat ramp. During whale season (December-April), the trip to Molokini often doubles as a bit of whale watching.

Plan to go early, as the wind and waves are calmest in the mornings. Trips to Molokini will sometimes be cancelled if the wind and the waves get too vigorous. Molokini is a very popular destination for visitors and can sometimes be crowded.

SOUTH MAUI SIGHTS, SHOPPING, AND DINING

Recommended Sights:
- Maui Brewing Company Tours - 605 Lipoa Parkway, Kihei
- Sunset at Keawakapu Beach - 2960 South Kihei Road, Kihei
- Wailea Beach Path - From the Fairmont Kea Lani, Wailea
- Snorkeling at Molokini

Recommended Shopping:
- Kihei Kalama Village (many local-crafted items) - 1941 South Kihei Road, Kihei
- The Shops at Wailea (upscale shops) - 3750 Wailea Alanui Drive, Wailea

Recommended Dining:
- 808 Deli (best sandwiches) - 2511 South Kihei Road, Suite 102, Kihei
- Eskimo Candy (seafood and deli) - 2665 Wai Wai Place, Kihei
- Cafe O'Lei (Hawaiian dining) - 2439 South Kihei Road, Kihei
- Monkeypod Kitchen (great for drinks) - 10 Wailea Gateway Place, Wailea
- Matteo's Osteria (Italian restaurant & wine bar) - 161 Wailea Ike Place, Suite A107, Wailea

- Humuhumunukunukuapua'a at Grand Wailea (fine dining) - 3850 Wailea Alanui Drive, Wailea

Step 4. WEST MAUI

MA'ALAEA

Ma'alaea is located about six miles south of Wailuku at the junction where the Honoapi'ilani Highway reaches the south coast. Many of Maui's dinner cruises, fishing tours, and snorkel excursions originate from Ma'alaea Harbor. During whale season (December through April), many whale watching boats also pick up passengers in Ma'alaea Harbor.

The Maui Ocean Center is also located in Ma'alaea Harbor. The nation's largest tropical reef aquarium, the Maui Ocean Center is dedicated to perpetuating and sharing Hawaiian culture, as well as conserving and sustaining Hawaii's marine life for future generations. The 750,000 gallon shark tank has over 20 sharks, which can be viewed from all angles inside the aquarium's 54 foot walk-through glass tunnel.

Ma'alaea also has several miles of secluded beaches, usually occupied only by the occasional fisherman or surfer. A few miles up the road from Ma'alaea (heading toward toward Lahaina) you will find Papawai Scenic Lookout, where visitors can often observe whales breaching during whale season.

LAHAINA

Lahaina is a popular location for visitors, with approximately two million people per year coming to see its sights. Lahaina's original name, Lele, means "relentless sun" in Hawaiian, referring to the extremely dry and sunny climate.

Lahaina has a very rich history. In 1802, King

Kamehameha built a brick palace in Lahaina, along with homes and other buildings, making Lahaina the capital of the Hawaiian Kingdom. The brick palace he built became the seat of government for the Hawaiian Kingdom until 1845. During the 1800s, Lahaina was a major whaling port and fishing town due to its favorable ocean conditions, dry weather, and location along whale migration routes. It has also been essential to the pineapple and sugar industries, and a place where many immigrants first landed in Maui.

Lahaina's oceanfront setting, warm weather, and walkable Front Street make it one of the most popular places on Maui to visit. As you stroll down Front Street you will find fine restaurants, bars, stores, and art galleries, all while enjoying the gorgeous ocean view. From December through April, visitors set sail from Lahaina Harbor on whale watching tours, as humpback whales come to frolic in the waters off the coast of Lahaina. Don't forget to try Hawaii's famous shave ice, perfect for cooling off in between exploring Front Street's shops and galleries.

Sunset in Lahaina is the perfect time and place for attending a traditional Hawaiian luau. Listen to live music, watch hula and other traditional dance performances, and look up at the stars while you feast on kalua pig cooked in an imu (an oven dug into the earth and lined with rocks and banana leaves), haupia (coconut pudding) and poi (taro). The Old Lahaina Luau is considered by many to be the best luau on Maui. Alternatively, The Feast at Lele offers a five course, sit-down Polynesian dinner if you want to forego the buffet line.

The Kapalua-West Maui Airport is a small regional airport that serves West Maui, including Lahaina, Ka'anapali, and Kapalua. Built in 1987, the

Kapalua-West Maui Airport is located about five miles from Lahaina.

KA'ANAPALI

Ka'anapali (meaning "rolling cliffs" in Hawaiian) is a beautiful resort town that historically served as a royal retreat for the rulers of Maui. Today, several major resorts and condo complexes line the three miles of Ka'anapali Beach, where visitors can enjoy the mild waves, sunny weather, and fine white sand.

Ka'anapali has multiple golf courses, combining world-class golfing with views of the ocean and West Maui Mountains. Other activities to enjoy in Ka'anapali include ziplining, cliff diving, snorkeling, and swimming. While in Ka'anapali, visit Whaler's Village, a beachside mall with boutiques, restaurants, a whaling museum, hula lessons and more.

North of Ka'anapali are the communities of Napili and Kapalua. Napili offers restaurants, a farmers' market, and Napili Bay. Kapalua was once a pineapple plantation that is now a 1500-acre resort.

WEST MAUI BEACHES

Please remember that all beaches in Maui have potential dangers. For more tips on beach safety, please read the section titled, "Important Information for Visitors."

LAHAINA BEACHES

Launiupoko Beach Park

The defining feature of Launiupoko Beach Park is the natural pool enclosed by a lava rock wall. The pool is a lovely shallow spot for little ones to play. This beach is a great place to lounge in the sun or go for a quick swim, but it is also excellent for for surfing, especially in the summer months. Enjoy the beautiful view of Lanai across the clear blue waters, visible even from the grassy areas beyond the beach. The wind doesn't usually kick up until later in the afternoon here, unlike many of Maui's other beaches – so if you have gotten a late start, head for Launiupoko Beach Park! One word of caution: be mindful and watch for coconuts that sometimes fall from the trees along this beach.

<u>Location:</u> Kai Hele Ku Street and Honoapi'ilani Highway, Lahaina

<u>Amenities:</u>
- Portable toilet
- Showers
- Picnic area

Puamana Beach Park

Puamana Beach Park is a rocky, rugged beach and therefore not the best for sunbathing or swimming, but it is excellent for beginners learning to surf, thanks to its small waves. Fishing is another favorite pastime at Puamana Beach Park. A popular Hawaiian song from 1937 called "Puamana" speaks of the area's beauty, and the moon glistening on the whispering waves.

<u>Location:</u> Near Mile Marker 9, Honoapi'ilani Highway, Lahaina

<u>Amenities:</u>
- Portable toilet
- Showers

- Picnic area

Shark Pit Beach (Makila Beach)

Shark Pit Beach is named after a part of the reef where several whitetip reef sharks are known to congregate. Whitetip reef sharks are rarely aggressive towards humans, though they may get close in order to give you a good inspection. Mainly spear fishers risk being bitten by whitetip reef sharks in an attempt to steal their catch! Surfing is a favorite activity at Shark Pit beach, but should only be attempted by very experienced surfers with knowledge of the area.

<u>Location:</u> Front Street and Shaw Street, Lahaina
<u>Amenities:</u>
- Shower

Baby Beach Lahaina (Pu'unoa Beach)

As the name implies, Baby Beach is a generally safe, family-friendly beach. It has a shallow lagoon that is protected from the waves by an exposed reef breakwater, and is perfect for small children to paddle and play in as parents watch them enjoy the gentle ocean waters. The winds can be strong in the afternoon here (as with most Maui beaches), so plan for an early beach day.

<u>Location:</u> Off Front Street at Pu'unoa Place, Lahaina
<u>Amenities:</u>
- Restrooms
- Shower

Wahikuli Beach Park and Hanakaoʻo Beach Park (Canoe Beach)

Wahikuli Beach Park is known as a great spot for surfing or snorkeling. The reef here creates enjoyable waves that are good for surfing in times of both light and heavy surf. Wahikuli means "noisy place" and while the name may have initially referred to the sound of crashing waves, it is now descriptive of the cars rushing by on the adjacent highway.

If the afternoon winds have spoiled your beach trip, consider heading to Hanakao'o Beach Park, north of Wahikuli. The cove of Hanakao'o protects beachgoers from the wind. It's not a great swimming beach, but it is a beautiful stretch of white sand with an unspoiled charm. Hanakao'o Beach also hosts outrigger canoe regattas throughout the year, so it has been given the nickname of Canoe Beach.

Location: Kaniau Road and Honoapi'ilani Highway, Lahaina

Amenities:
- Restrooms
- Showers
- Lifeguard (at Hanakao'o)
- Picnic area

Kahekili Beach Park

Kahekili Beach Park was named for Maui's last ali'i (ruler), King Kahekili ("The Thunderer"). For beginner snorkelers and divers, Kahekili Beach Park is the best beach to test out your skills. A reef is located close to the shoreline of this beach, making snorkeling

exceptionally easy. You will want to start swimming right away on entering the water, so as not to step on the reefs. While snorkeling at Kahekili Beach Park, you will commonly encounter Hawaiian green sea turtles in additional to a wide variety of tropical fish. During whale season (December-April), you can often view humpback whales from this beach, and even hear them underwater!
<u>Location:</u> Kai Ala Drive, Lahaina
<u>Amenities:</u>
- Restrooms
- Showers
- Picnic area

KA'ANAPALI AND UPPER WEST BEACHES

Ka'anapali Beach

Ka'anapali Beach is a stunning resort beach stretching three miles long, with pure golden-white sands and gentle ocean waves. Ka'anapali Beach is well known for its picturesque beauty and for its great snorkeling and easy swimming. The beach is also conveniently located within walking distance to many restaurants and other attractions. Soft sand, turquoise water, and plenty of ocean activities like stand up paddle boarding, snorkeling, surfing, boogie boarding, and parasailing make this a world-class beach.

Ka'anapali Beach is also known for the cliff jumping that takes place off the volcanic rock cliff known as Black Rock, or Pu'u Keka'a. Every evening at sunset, a cliff diver lights the torches along the cliff, then dives off of Black

Rock in a reenactment of the legendary athletic feat performed by King Kahekili, ruler of Maui and Oahu in the 1700s.

Black Rock is a beautiful and rugged spot, but it can also be dangerous. Both cliff divers and snorkelers have perished in the ocean surrounding Black Rock. Never jump from Black Rock without watching exactly where others have jumped first – you don't want to jump into reefs or shallow water! Many people think of snorkeling as an easy activity, but it can actually be very strenuous – especially in places with strong currents (such as Black Rock). For more information about beach safety, please refer to the section "Important Information for Visitors."

<u>Location:</u> Along three miles of Ka'anapali Parkway, Ka'anapali
<u>Amenities:</u>
- Restrooms nearby
- Showers

Napili Bay

Napili Bay is definitely one of the most beautiful beaches in Maui. It's not visible from the street, but due to its popularity, you can find it by looking for the cars parked nearby. The calm waters and soft sand lend a sleepy quality to this gorgeous West Maui beach.

<u>Location:</u> Napili Place, Napili
<u>Amenities:</u>
- Showers

Kapalua Bay Beach

Kapalua Bay Beach is a remarkably

beautiful beach, with the perfect crescent shape to keep waves gentle. The vibrant sea life in this tropical paradise makes it a wonderful spot for snorkeling. Palm trees and grassy lawn backing the beach provide a relaxing sanctuary to nap or have a picnic. Kapalua Bay Beach is also an excellent beach for families with small children.
Location: Bay Drive, Kapalua (near the Montage Resort)
Amenities:
- Restrooms
- Showers
- Lifeguard
- Picnic area

Oneloa Bay Beach

Oneloa Bay Beach is an pristine, uncrowded, quarter-mile long beach next to the Ritz Carlton. The ocean fronting the beach has a reef at the right, extending to the middle – but has a nice sandy bottom on the left side. So you will want to snorkel to the right and swim to the left for the best experience. Only snorkel and swim on calm days, as rip currents sometimes occur here when the surf is strong.
Note: Big Beach in Makena is also sometimes referred to as Oneloa Beach – so if you're meeting friends, be sure to ask which Oneloa Beach they're referring to!
Location: Ironwood Lane, Kapalua
Amenities:
- Showers

D.T. Fleming Beach Park

This beach is named after David Thomas

Fleming, the man who helped create a successful pineapple industry on Maui. This world-class beach has a long, golden stretch of sand with a backdrop of ironwood trees for shade. D.T. Fleming Beach is less developed than Ka'anapali Beach, although it does have amenities such as showers and restrooms. Strong waves and powerful rip currents can make D.T. Fleming Beach dangerous at times, so be aware of surf conditions.
<u>Location:</u> Mile Marker 31, Honoapi'ilani Highway, Kapalua
<u>Amenities:</u>
- Restrooms
- Showers
- Lifeguard
- Picnic area

Mokule'ia Bay (Slaughterhouse Beach)
Slaughterhouse Beach is not the most appealing name, however this beach was named not for killer waves but for a slaughterhouse that was once located nearby. To reach this beach, you will need to walk down a few flights of stairs, so be prepared and don't bring too much gear with you! Morning is the best time for snorkeling here, with plenty of Hawaiian green sea turtles, eels, and octopus to be seen. Mokule'ia Bay has lots of soft sand, shady areas, and a "hideaway" feeling that will convince you that you've found paradise.
<u>Location:</u> Off Honoapi'ilani Highway (east of D.T. Fleming Beach and west of Honolua Bay), Kapalua
<u>Amenities:</u>

- Picnic area

Honolua Bay

Honolua means "two harbors" in Hawaiian. This huge bay often has murky water at the shoreline, especially after rains. This is due to a stream that travels through agricultural areas before emptying into the ocean here in Honolua Bay. The snorkeling is better further out in the bay. Unfortunately, this area is notorious for thieves breaking into cars, so don't leave any valuables in your vehicle, and consider leaving it unlocked so thieves don't break the windows to see what's inside.
Location: Between Mile Marker 32 and 33, Honoapi'ilani Highway, Kapalua
Amenities:
- Portable toilet

Nakalele Point and Nakalele Blowhole
The prime attraction of the Nakalele Point is the blowhole, a hole in the ground that periodically erupts with a geyser-like jet of water shooting into the air. It is particularly impressive (and dangerous) during high surf. The blowhole has caused several deaths, mostly visitors who have gotten too close to the blowhole and were sucked in by retreating water. Currently there is only one warning sign in the area, partly because of a dispute about who owns the land (the state or Maui Land & Pineapple Company). Take heed and only view the blowhole from afar, for your own safety.
Location: Between Mile Markers 38 and 39,

Honoapi'ilani Highway, Lahaina
<u>Amenities:</u>
- No facilities

WEST MAUI SIGHTS, SHOPPING, AND DINING

Recommended Sights:
- Maui Ocean Center - 192 Ma'alaea Road, Ma'alaea
- Whale Watching (December-April), - Papawai Scenic Lookout, Ma'alaea (and other spots)
- Baldwin Home Museum - 120 Dickenson Street, Lahaina
- Lahaina Banyan Tree (planted in 1873, 60 feet tall) - Front Street & Canal Street, Lahaina

Recommended Shopping:
- Front Street Oceanfront Shops - Front Street, Lahaina
- Lahaina Civic Center Craft Fair (Sundays) - 1840 Honoapi'ilani Highway, Lahaina
- Lahaina Cannery Mall (enclosed, air conditioning) - 1221 Honoapi'ilani Highway, Lahaina
- The Outlets of Maui (validated parking with purchase) - 900 Front Street, Lahaina
- Whalers Village - 2435 Ka'anapali Parkway, Ka'anapali

Recommended Dining:
- Lahaina Grill (voted best Lahaina restaurant) - 127 Lahainaluna Road, Lahaina
- Koa's Seaside Grill (steak dinner here at sunset!) - 839 Front Street, Lahaina

- Aloha Mixed Plate (local style food) - 1285 Front Street, Lahaina
- Slappy Cakes (decadent breakfast) - 3350 Lower Honoapi'ilani Road, Suite 701, Lahaina
- Japengo (Pacific Rim fare & sushi) at the Hyatt - 200 Nohea Kai Drive, Ka'anapali
- Merriman's (Hawaiian fine dining) - 1 Bay Club Place, Kapalua

Step 5. UPCOUNTRY MAUI AND HALEAKALA

Makawao

The area known as Upcountry Maui is located on the slopes of Haleakala, where cooler temperatures and lush vegetation make a welcome change from the beach. Upcountry is a unique country paradise made up of cattle ranches, farms, bright green horse pastures, and homes – all with a backdrop of thick foliage, eucalyptus trees, and tropical flowers. Right in the middle of it all is Makawao, a small paniolo town (Hawaiian cowboy town), with its quaint shopping area full of wooden storefronts and old-Hawaii charm.

The Makawao Parade and Rodeo have been held each Fourth of July for over 50 years. Shop Maui Hands to bring home a unique souvenir or gift made by a Maui artisan. Visit the No'eau Visual Arts Center, where you can take art classes or enjoy the free gallery exhibits. Don't forget to stop at T Komoda's store & Bakery, Hawaii's best bakery since 1916. They sell out early and are also closed on Wednesdays and Sundays, but a donut stick or a cream puff from Komoda's may be the highlight of your entire trip to Maui! The combination of its paniolo heritage, its artistic scene, and the cooler Upcountry temperatures make Makawao a must-see town.

Kula

Kula means "open meadows" in Hawaiian. The rolling hills and rich volcanic soil of Kula are where much of Maui's local produce is grown, including sweet maui onions, tomatoes, and strawberries. Kula also produces spectacular "pin-cushion" proteas and other tropical flowers.

The Ali'i Kula Lavender Farm is a relaxing and tranquil way to spend an Upcountry afternoon, while escaping the heat of the beach. "Ali'i" means royal, and the stunning bicoastal ocean views are certainly fit for royalty. Many varieties of fragrant lavender will usually be in bloom at the farm, which also grows proteas, hydrangeas, roses, and native Hawaiian plants. This lovely farm is worth a visit, if only for the scenic photos you'll take. Sample some lavender tea or delicious lavender scones with lilikoi jam in the unique gift shop and cafe.

Ocean Vodka Organic Farm and Distillery is located in Kula, as well as Surfing Goat Dairy, and both offer fun and informative tours. The Maui Wine Ulupalakua Vineyards offers a free tour and complimentary tasting, and the Ulupalakua Ranch Store next door serves a wonderful lunch with lamb, beef and elk from the Ranch, located nearby on the slopes of Haleakala.

Haiku

Haiku was once a bustling pineapple plantation with two canneries (Haiku Cannery and Pauwela Cannery), until the main refinery moved to Kahului. Today, this country town has a few restaurants and shops located where Kokomo Road and Haiku Road meet. Like Paia and the North Shore, the hippie culture has taken root in Haiku and the town has a distinctive Bohemian vibe.

Haleakala

Sunrise at Haleakala Crater is one of the most

popular activities in Upcountry Maui. Plan to get started in the wee hours – it can take two hours to drive to the summit of Haleakala, and you will want to arrive at the Haleakala Visitor Center by half an hour before sunrise. Sunrise happens between 5:30am-6:50am, depending on season. It gets very cold at the summit of Haleakala (in the 40s is common) so dress warmly in layers, and bring blankets with you. Your efforts will be rewarded with a stunning sunrise, unbelievable panoramic views, and native plants and birds that exist only here at the top of Maui's dormant volcano.

UPCOUNTRY MAUI SIGHTS, SHOPPING, AND DINING

Recommended Sights:
- Makawao Forest Reserve (easy, gorgeous hiking) - Kahakapao Loop, Makawao
- Ali'i Kula Lavender Farm - 11 Waipoli Road, Kula
- Surfing Goat Dairy - 3651 Omaopio Road, Kula
- Ocean Vodka Organic Farm and Distillery - 4051 Omaopio Road, Kula
- Temple of Peace Healing Sanctuary - 575 Haiku Road, haiku

Recommended Shopping:
- Makawao Crossroads (shops and galleries) - Makawao and Baldwin Avenues, Makawao
- Upcountry Farmer's Market (Tuesdays and Saturdays) - 55 Kiopaa Street, Makawao
- Haiku Marketplace - 810 Haiku Road, Haiku

Recommended Dining:

- Makawao Steak House (a staple for 40 years) - 3612 Baldwin Avenue, Makawao
- T Komoda's Store and Bakery (donuts and pastries) - 3674 Baldwin Avenue, Makawao
- Ulupalakua Ranch Store (casual) - 14800 Pi'ilani Highway, Kula
- La Provence (French cuisine) - 3158 Lower Kula Road, Kula
- Mediterranean Grill Food Truck (lamb gyros, local produce) - 810 Haiku Road, Haiku
- Hali'imaile General Store (finest dining) - 900 Hali'imaile Road, Hali'imaile (near Makawao)

Step 6. ROAD TO HANA AND SOUTHEAST MAUI

The Road to Hana

The Road to Hana on Maui is considered one of the world's most picturesque drives. This drive is more than just a way to get to your destination – the journey is the important part. This curvy coastal cliff road has amazing ocean views, rainforest, and waterfalls. Although it is a paved road, you will encounter many single-lane bridges and over 600 hairpin curves, so be ready! The speed limit averages 25 mph, meaning the drive takes a minimum of 2 and a half hours without traffic.

To prepare for your Road to Hana excursion (assuming you're not taking a van tour, which is the easiest way to experience it), pack food, plenty of water, a fully charged phone and camera, some towels, good hiking shoes, and insect repellent. Bring enough cash to buy items from local food vendors, but leave valuables behind. Fill up your gas tank and head out early, as you don't want to accidentally end up driving the Road to Hana in the dark!

The Destinations

There are at least 15 worthwhile stops to make on the Road to Hana, but you couldn't visit them all in one day (especially because you don't want to be driving back on this winding road at night). Researching which stops to make along the Road to Hana can be more exhausting than actually driving it, so here are five recommendations to start with – an assortment of unique beaches, waterfalls, and cultural sites, while skipping the most inaccessible or dangerous stops.

Twin Falls

The hike to see Twin Falls is easy and very beautiful. There are multiple waterfalls, and several areas to swim at. These are the first waterfalls on the Road to Hana, and since they are fairly easy to access, the hike can sometimes be a little crowded. The farm stand at the front sells delicious coconut candy, refreshing smoothies, and local coconuts cut open with a machete for you to enjoy the fresh coconut juice. During rain the Twin Falls area can have flash floods, so obey all warning signs.

Kahanu Garden and Pi'ilanihale Heiau

The Kahanu Garden and Preserve is home to 300 varieties of taro and 120 varieties of breadfruit, preserved here as part of Hawaiian culture and history. The Pi'ilanihale Heiau is the largest heiau (Polynesian temple) in the world and is an impressive lava rock structure that took over 300 years to build. It is nearly 50 feet high, and the size of two football fielzs.

Wai'anapanapa (Black Sand Beach)

Wai'anapanapa State Park includes Pa'iloa Beach, also known as Black Sand Beach. The black sand was created when a lava flow happened at this beach several hundred years ago. The stunning pictures you'll take here will likely be the most treasured photos of your trip to Maui!

Hana Bay Beach Park

Hana Bay Beach Park is a nice, safe beach with welcome amenities such as restrooms and showers, so it's a good place to stretch your legs. This beautiful beach has gentle waves and good snorkeling, as well as Tutu's Snack Shop, one of the only places in Hana to grab a bite to eat. This is the perfect place to take a break before pushing on to the Seven Sacred Pools, or simply heading back. But keep going to the next stop – you won't regret it!

'O'he'o Gulch (Seven Sacred Pools)
The Seven Sacred Pools in Kipahulu is one of the most magical places on the island of Maui, with beautiful tiered pools created by waterfalls. There are more than seven pools – many more when water levels are high. In good weather you may swim in these tranquil pools, which are fed by inland streams. Some areas are known for dangerous rock slides, so be sure to obey all warning signs.

ROAD TO HANA SIGHTS, SHOPPING, AND DINING

Recommended Sights:
- Twin Falls - Mile Marker 2, Hana Highway, haiku
- Kahanu Garden and Pi'ilanihale Heiau - Mile Marker 31, Hana Highway, Hana
- Wai'anapanapa (Black Sand Beach) - Mile Marker 32, Hana Highway, Hana
- Hana Bay Beach Park - 150 Keawa Place, Hana
- 'O'he'o Gulch (Seven Sacred Pools) - Mile Marker 42, Hana Highway, Kipahulu

Recommended Shopping:

- Hasegawa General Store (quirky and iconic, est. 1910) – 5165 Hana Highway, Hana

Recommended Dining:
- My Thai, at Nahiku Marketplace – Mile Marker 29, Hana
- Tutu's Snack Shop – Hana Bay Beach Park, Hana

Step 7. MAUI ACTIVITIES AND ADVENTURES

Ocean Activities and Adventures

Whale Watching Tours: Maui is the foremost whale-watching destination of the Hawaiian Islands. Most tours depart from Ma'alaea but some also originate in Lahaina.

Sunset Dinner Cruise: Cruises depart from Ma'alaea or Lahaina.

Surfing or Stand Up Paddleboarding: Surfboards or paddleboards can be rented at lots of shops. Consider booking lessons to make your trip truly memorable.

Boogie Boarding or Body Surfing: While you can rent a boogie board, you might be better off just purchasing one, then hitting up D.T. Fleming Beach in Kapalua for the best waves.

Parasailing: Maui's professional parasailing companies make it fun for people of all ages and abilities to learn.

Kiteboarding and Windsurfing Lessons: Multiple schools offer kiteboarding and windsurfing lessons on Maui, mainly in the Kahului area.

Snorkeling Trip to Molokini: Several charters offer trips to Molokini for snorkeling, departing from Kihei.

Scuba Diving: Scuba tours are available for experienced divers, as well as lessons for those who want to learn.

Sport Fishing: Maui's sport fishing charter companies depart from Kihei or Lahaina areas.

Kayaking: Whether you take a kayaking tour or rent your own kayak, there are many spots along Maui's shoreline to go kayaking.

Air Activities and Adventures

Helicopter Tours: Some of Maui's most inaccessible areas can only be viewed by helicopter. Tours depart from the Kahului Airport.

Ziplining: Experience Maui from above on a tropical zip line! Zip lines on the North Shore, Central Maui, Ka'anapali and Kapalua mean you have several adventures to choose from.

Paragliding: With paragliding lessons at Waipoli FlightPark in Kula, you can fly tandem with an instructor and experience the freedom of soaring through the sky.

Flight Lessons: Maui Flight Academy offers day trip lessons from Kahului Airport. Fly over a volcano, or to a neighboring island!

Land Activities and Adventures

- Luau (Old Lahaina Luau in Lahaina is best rated)
- Sunrise at Haleakala National Park
- Maui Tropical Plantation, Wailuku
- Ali'i Kula Lavender Farm, Kula
- Alexander & Baldwin Sugar Museum, Kahului
- Ocean Vodka Organic Farm and Distillery, Kula
- Maui Wine Ulupalakua Vineyards, Ulupalakua
- Maui Ocean Center, Ma'alaea
- Golfing at numerous golf courses in Wailea, Lahaina, Ka'anapali and more
- Iao Valley State Park, Wailuku
- Spa Day (Ho'omana Spa Maui in Makawao is best rated)
- Hiking (Makawao Forest Reserve; Pipiwai Trail, Kipahulu; Haleakala Summit)
- Bailey House and Museum, Wailuku
- Charles Lindbergh's Grave at Palapala Ho'omau Church, Kipahulu
- Kula Botanical Gardens, Kula
- Maui Brewing Company Tour, Kihei
- Burn'n Love Elvis Impersonation Show at Maui Theater, Lahaina
- Horseback Riding Tours, Upcountry Maui
- Mountain Biking Down Haleakala
- Shave Ice: It's not just a dessert treat, it's an experience! Local tropical flavors over soft snow-like shaved ice makes this a memorable moment. Ululani's Hawaiian Shave Ice is best rated, and they have locations in Lahaina, Kahului, Maui Lani, and Kihei.

About the Expert

Dena Gray is a writer and graphic artist who lives in Upcountry, Maui with her husband and two children. After moving to Maui in 2010, she set out to learn all there was to know about this island paradise she now calls home. She has put her many exciting adventures (and occasional mishaps!) to use, frequently guiding family and friends visiting from the mainland to make sure they have the trip of a lifetime. Directing you to the best beaches and most awe-inspiring waterfalls, as well as the best shave ice on the island, Dena shares with you how to enjoy Maui to the fullest!

For more 'how to' tips, visit www.HowExpert.com.

Recommended Resources

www.HowExpert.com - HowExpert publishes quick 'how to' guides in unique topics by everyday people who want to share their passions/talents/expertise to the world.

Made in the USA
Lexington, KY
04 January 2018